Beacon Small-Group Bible Studies

Hebrews

Beacon Small-Group Bible Studies

HEBREWS

He Is Here—At Last

by

Gene Van Note

Beacon Hill Press of Kansas City
Kansas City, Missouri

ISBN: 0-8341-0623-X

ISBN: 0-8341-0624-8 (Set Number)

Printed in the United States of America

Cover Photo: H. Armstrong Roberts

Permission to quote from the following copyrighted versions of the Bible is acknowledged with appreciation:

The Holy Bible, New International Version (NIV), copyright © 1978 by New York International
    Bible Society.

The *New American Standard Bible* (NASB), © The Lockman Foundation, 1960, 1962, 1968,
    1971, 1972, 1973, 1975.

The New Testament: A Private Translation in the Language of the People (Williams), by Charles
    B. Williams; copyright 1937 by Bruce Humphries, Inc.; copyright assigned 1949 to the
    Moody Bible Institute of Chicago.

Unless otherwise noted all Scripture quotations in this study are from the *New International
    Version.*

Contents

HOW TO USE THIS STUDY GUIDE

Before You Begin This Adventure in a
Small-Group Bible Study...
Read These Pages of Introduction

God has created us with a basic human need for close personal relationships. This may take place *as you gather in a small group* to apply the Bible to your life.

I. What Should Happen in Small-Group Bible Study?

"They devoted themselves to the apostles' teaching and to the fellowship ... and to prayer" (Acts 2:42, NIV).

Each group is different ... yet all should include three kinds of activity—

DISCUSSION BIBLE STUDY
SHARING EXPERIENCES
PRAYING TOGETHER

The time you spend in Bible study, sharing, and praying will vary according to the needs of the group. However, do not neglect any of these activities.

The Bible contains God's plan for our salvation and gives us His guidance for our lives. Keep the focus on God speaking to you from His Word.

On the other hand, just to learn "Bible facts" will make little difference in a person's life. To give opportunity for persons to *share* what the truth means to them is to "let God come alive today." Learn to listen intently to others and to share what you feel God's Word is saying to you.

Allow time for *prayer*. Personal communion with God is essential in all fruitful Bible studies. Determine to make prayer more than a "nod to God" at the beginning or end of each session. As members participate in sincere, unhurried prayer—you will be amazed how God's power will meet needs in your group ... today!

II. How to Begin Your First Session Together

The leader of a new group may wish to prepare name tags with first and last names large enough to be seen plainly.

It is important to order the *Beacon Small-Group Bible Study* guides and give one to each person in your group at the beginning of the first session. Pass out the guides and refer the group to this section of the Introduction. Then ask each person to consider the following:

One thing I would like to gain from sharing in this time together is:

Rank the following in order using number one (1) to indicate the most important and number five (5) the least important.

(   ) 1. Learning to know Bible truths and apply them to my life.
(   ) 2. A chance to begin all over again in my spiritual life.
(   ) 3. To grow in my personal faith in God.
(   ) 4. To deepen my friendships with others in the group as we study the
           Word together.
(   ) 5. Other purpose _____

Take time to go around the group to introduce yourselves. Then let each member share what he or she would like to gain from this Bible study by filling in the blanks and by discussing this statement: I chose _____ as number one because _____. I put _____ as number five because _____.

At this point, pause for prayer, asking God to bless this Bible study and especially to meet the needs just expressed by the members of the group.

III. A Key to Success . . . Make a Group Commitment

What should be included in the group commitment? At the first or second meeting, read the following points, then discuss each one separately.

1. Agree to make regular attendance a top priority of the group.

    Commitment to each other is of vital importance.

2. Where and when will the group meet?

    Decide on a place and time. The place can be always in the same home or in a different home each week, at a restaurant, or in any other relaxed setting. Plan to be on time.

    The time _____ the place(s) _____
    How often?   (   ) Every week
                         (   ) Every other week

3. Decide on the length of the meetings.

    The minimum should be one hour—maximum two hours. Whatever you decide, be sure to dismiss on time. Those who wish may remain after the group is dismissed. Length _____.

4. Decide whether the same person will lead each session, or if you prefer a group coordinator and a rotation of leaders.

    Our leader or coordinator is _____.

5. Agree together that there shall be no criticism of others. Also no discussion of church problems, and no gossip shall be expressed in the group. Our goal in this Bible study is to affirm and to build up each other.

6. Decide on the maximum number of people your group should contain. When this number is reached you will encourage the formation of a new group. We want our group to grow. Newcomers, as they understand and agree to the group commitment, will keep things fresh. Feel free to bring a

friend. Whenever our group reaches an average attendance of _____ persons for three consecutive weeks, we will plan to begin a new group.

Do not become a closed clique. This would eventually lead to an ingrown group. Our goal is outreach, friendliness, and openness to new people.

7. Our time together as a group will be more fulfilling if all of us complete our personal Bible reading before we come together again.

Are group members deciding to make this commitment to personal Bible reading and reflection? _____

8. Decide on the number of times you wish to meet before you reevaluate the areas of your commitment. (Enter below)

MY COMMITMENT TO CHRIST
and THE MEMBERS OF MY GROUP

I agree to meet with others in my group for _____ weeks to become a learner in God's Word.

I commit myself to give priority to our group gatherings, to a thoughtful reading of the Bible passages to be explored, and to love and support others in my group.

Signed _____ Date _____

IV. Guidelines

1. Get acquainted with each other; get on a first-name basis.
2. Each one bring your Bible and keep it open during the study.
3. As you read the Bible passage, each person may ask himself three questions:
   —What does the passage say?
   —What does it mean?
   —What does it mean to me?
4. Stay with the Bible passage before you. Moving to numerous cross references may confuse a person new to the Bible.
5. Avoid technical theological words. Make sure any theological terms you use are explained clearly to the group.
6. The leader or coordinator should prepare for each session by studying the passage thoroughly before the group meeting, including reviewing the

questions in the study guide. In the group study, the leader should ask the study guide questions, giving adequate time for the discussion of each question.

Remember, the leader is not to lecture on what he has learned from studying, but should lead the group in discovering for themselves what the scripture says. In sharing your discoveries say, "The scripture says," rather than, "My church says..."

7. The leader should not talk too much and should not answer his own questions. The leader should give opportunity for anyone who wishes to speak. Redirect some of the questions back to the group. As they get to know each other better, the discussion will move more freely.

The flow of discussion in an effective group looks like this:

And not like this:

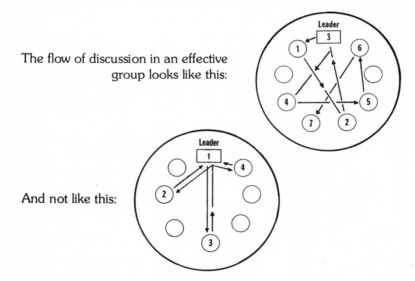

8. In a loving and firm manner maintain the guidelines for the group. Discourage overtalkative members from monopolizing the time. If necessary, the leader may speak privately to the overtalkative one and enlist his aid in encouraging all to participate. Direct questions to all persons in the group.

9. Plan to reserve some time at the end of each session for prayer together. Encourage any who wish to lead out in spoken prayer in response to the scripture truths or personal needs expressed in the group.

Even if you do not complete all the study for that particular meeting, *take time to pray.* The main purpose of group Bible study is not just to cover all the facts, but to apply the truth to human lives. It will be exciting to discover your lives growing and changing as you encourage each other in Christ's love.

A highly effective way to pray in a group like this is "conversationally." "Conversational" prayer includes:

    a. Each group member who wishes to do so tells God frankly what he has to say to Him.

    b. Praying is in a conversational tone—directly, simply, briefly.

    c. Only one thing is prayed about at a time—a personal concern.

    d. Once a group member has introduced his concern, at least one other member, and probably several, by audible prayer "covers with love" their friend's concern.

    e. Then there is a waiting in silence before God. Each person listens to what God is saying to him.

    f. Following the listening period, another member may introduce a personal concern in prayer. The prayer time continues with members feeling free to pray several times.

V. Aids for Your Study

For Group Leaders

You will find helpful, *How to Lead a Small-Group Bible Study,* by Gene Van Note, available from the Beacon Hill Press of Kansas City, Box 527, Kansas City, MO 64141.

For Leaders, Coordinators, and Participants

Bible commentaries should not be taken with you to the Bible study, but it is often helpful to refer to sound commentaries and expositions in your preparation. We recommend:

Beacon Bible Commentary
    Volume 10—Hebrews—Revelation

Beacon Bible Expositions
    Volume 11—Hebrews, James, Peter

It is also helpful to refer occasionally to some general Bible resources, such as:

    Know Your New Testament, by Ralph Earle
    Halley's Bible Handbook

The above resources are available from Beacon Hill Press of Kansas City or from your publishing house.

—This introduction by Wil M. Spaite

As I enter your holy presence, Lord,
in this quiet room
I find it hard to imagine
the great temple, the smoking sacrifice,
the lambs and kids awaiting slaughter,
the knives, the blood, the solemn ceremony
of life poured out
to take away your people's sins.

What a hard lesson it must be for men to learn
if over many centuries
this was the way you showed yourself a holy God.
And so I thank you for this
new covenant; this new and living way.

It is, I recognize, still by blood.
I come, as they come, only by sacrifice.
But my Lamb of Sacrifice is Jesus.
Upon His sacred head I lay my sins.
    O Lord, my God and Father,
no wonder guilt lies heavy on the heart,
recognized or unrecognized,
of modern man!
If all that ritual of blood could never purge man's guilt,
but only point to Christ the Lamb of God,
how can any man be free of guilt
gnawing unnoticed in the secret places of his soul?

Only through Christ:
but perfectly through Him.
He is the true and living way, the sin-bearer, and
the Risen Savior.
In Him I rest and I rejoice.

Amen.

From *Someone Who Beckons*, by Timothy Dudley-Smith. © Timothy Dudley-Smith 1978 and used by permission of InterVarsity Press.

Introduction

Sometime during the second half of the first century, an unknown individual corresponded with some of his Christian friends. We do not know who he was, who they were, or the date his letter was sent. All we know about these questions is what we can infer from reading what the author wrote, and that is not enough to give precise answers.

The communication to which we refer is what we have come to know as the Book of Hebrews. It is immediately evident that it was not written as a book, nor does it have much in common with a letter you might write home to your parents, or to the other letters that form much of the New Testament. It has the characteristics of a pastoral letter, the kind a spiritual leader would send to his people, or as a pastor might give guidance to his congregation on an important doctrinal subject.

The Book of Hebrews is a carefully reasoned argument to show that Jesus Christ is the fulfillment of the Old Testament—not only its prophecy, but also its ritual. It is the firm conviction of the writer that all of the ritual and sacrifice of the ancient Jewish faith find their completion in the person of Jesus Christ.

The author, whoever he was, was obviously a highly trained scholar with a clear and complete understanding of Hebrew forms of worship. His readers, also, knew the meaning of the symbolism of the worship that took place in the Tabernacle and later in the Temple. It seems quite likely that they were Hebrew Christians. There are many indications that this letter was written because such Christians were being severely tempted to return to the life they knew before they confessed their faith in the Lord Jesus Christ. This has led many scholars to conclude that the letter was written in a persecution period just prior to the destruction of Jerusalem in A.D. 70.

The identity of the writer has been the subject of debate from very early in the history of the Christian faith. Probably the comment of the third-century Christian scholar, Origen, is as perceptive as any that have come later. He wrote, "Who it was that wrote the Epistle, God only knows."

There is no debate as to the significance of what this unknown author wrote. The product of his pen constitutes some of the most important doctrinal statements, combined with some of the most inspirational writing in the New Testament. Unfortunately, it is not well-known to our generation. The reason is evident; it is not all easy reading. Apparently, some of it was difficult even for the first readers. Its study, however, is worth the effort.

This exploration is designed for the beginner, for the person who does not have a large store of knowledge about Old Testament rituals and ceremonies. It will provide a relatively simple study guide to probe beneath the surface of this great book. When you are finished, some questions will remain. But once you have begun to catch the powerful message of this letter, you will find yourself returning again and again to its pages.

So, with a simple prayer for the Holy Spirit to give you spiritual insight, open the Bible and begin to read. Use any translation of the Bible with which you are comfortable. Unless otherwise indicated, this study guide is based on the *New International Version*. May the Lord grant you many happy times filled with joy and surprise in your study of the Book of Hebrews.

—Gene Van Note

1   He Is Here—At Last!

HEBREWS 1:1-14

As noted in the introduction, the Book of Hebrews came from the pen of an unknown writer. Nor can the date be circled on the calendar. There is no mystery, however, in the purpose of the book: "in these last days he [God] has spoken to us by his Son" (v. 2).

The first four verses of chapter 1 are a preface. They represent, in miniature, what the author intendes to discuss in the 13 chapters that follow:

—the time for waiting is over; Christ has come

—the need for repeated sacrifice is passed, Christ has completed our salvation

—a new age has dawned; the Messiah is here—at last!

The message of Hebrews is one of comparisons. The superiority of Christ over the Old Testament is the writer's first word. Christ is greater than the prophets through whom God spoke. Jesus revealed the Father more through His nature than with His words.

Our Lord is also demonstrated to be superior to the angels. The Jews of Christ's day believed that God was too far away from them to be reached with human words or abilities. They needed someone to speak to God for them. They were convinced that the angels bridged this gap.

Thus, the two great concepts of Hebrews surface in chapter 1: (1) Christ is the great Mediator, superior to all who preceded Him; and (2) Like no one else, He speaks to men for God, and to God in behalf of men.

Here is a simple outline of chapter 1:

1:1-4—One sentence that proclaims Christ's superiority
1:5-14—Five reasons that illustrate His greatness

Lesson Development

I. ONE SENTENCE (1:1-4)

A. Read these verses from several translations. The NASB has, as an alternate marginal reading for "in these last days" (v. 2), "at the end of these days."

B. Many scholars believe that the NASB marginal reading gives us the best clue as to the mood of the writer. If that is true, what was his attitude (toward God, man, and salvation)?

C. Compare the revelation of God *through* the prophets and the revelation *in* Christ. On the left below are some words that describe the prophets, their time, and ministry. Add any descriptive words you wish. In the other column, write in the difference in Christ's revelation.

Through the Prophets	*In Christ*
temporary	
preparatory	
ceremonial	
partial	

When you compare the prophets and Christ, what do you think is the most important difference?

Why, do you suppose, God chose to have Christ come when He did? Why "in these last days" did the Father decide to speak through His Son?

D. What was the Son's primary activity as noted in verse 3? Did He have to be the Son of God in order to accomplish it?

Do you see any special significance in the words, "He sat down at the right hand of the Majesty in heaven" (v. 3)? As you recall the Old Testament, what did Jesus do that the prophets did not, or could not, do? In what ways does that difference affect you?

E. Verses 1-4 are one sentence, the best classical Greek in the New Testament. The anonymous writer of Hebrews was, obviously, well-trained in the Greek language. When He became a Christian he did not go back to his childhood writing style. He used his talent and training for the Lord.

What talents and skills do you have that can be used in ministry for Christ?

II. FIVE REASONS (1:5-14)

A. Read verses 5-14.

B. There are at least five reasons given in these verses to show that Christ is superior to the angels. List them and the scripture verse in which they occur:

1.

2.

3.

4.

5.

C. Why do you think the author emphasizes the fact that the Son is superior to the angels?

Consider these questions along with the one above:

(1) What is the most important difference in the Son's and the angels' relationship to us?

(2) Could we make it without the angels as "ministering spirits" (v. 14)?

(3) Could we make it without the ministry of the Son, Jesus Christ? What would be the result if Christ's presence were taken from the earth?

III. A SECOND LOOK

A. What is the most encouraging verse in chapter 1?

B. What is the most challenging verse?

C. What verse is the most difficult to understand?

During each session list any verses you do not understand. Occasionally refer back to them to see if further study has cleared up any of your questions.

IV. PRAYER TIME

A. Select one new idea about Jesus Christ and thank the Lord for its impact on your life.

B. Think of the part of your life where the Lord seems to be the farthest away. Pray that some bridges will be built for Him to come to you.

C. Remember one person, or family, that seems cut off from God's love. Focus your prayerful concern on them.

D. Ask the Lord to help you find ways of ministering this week to the special needs of someone in your Bible study group.

V. SOMETHING TO THINK ABOUT OR DO

Your appreciation of the superiority of Christ over the angels will be increased by a look at the angels in the Bible. Here are some scriptures that will give you a place to begin your work:

Old Testament: Josh. 5:14 ff.; Judg. 13:26; 1 Kings 22:19; 2 Kings 19:35-36; Ps. 8:5; Isa. 6:1; Dan. 8:16; 9:21.

New Testament: Matt. 1:20; 4:11; Luke 2:6 ff.; 22:43.

2   Pay Attention, Jesus Is One of Us

HEBREWS 2:1-18

Introduction

"Therefore."

That word at the beginning of chapter 2 makes it clear that the Book of Hebrews is not a "stream of consciousness" report. Nor is it the disconnected memory of an old man. It is a carefully reasoned presentation of the meaning of Christ's death on the Cross. In the Gospel accounts of the life of our Lord, certain narratives might be deleted without destroying the message of salvation. Even if we never knew about the lovely incident at the marriage at Cana, Christ would still be our Savior. Our desire is not to erase anything from the Sacred Record, just to note that in relation to our redemption, not every incident is of equal value.

The Book of Hebrews is, by contrast, a single piece. You can benefit by reading verses, or chapters, separately. However, the power of the writer's message is most clearly seen when each part is related to the whole.

This is more difficult for us than it was for first-century Hebrew Christians. Sometimes we must struggle to find how the parts fit together. But it is worth it, for the completed picture is the most powerful portrait of Christ to be found in the New Testament.

"We must pay more careful attention, therefore" (2:1). The writer's logic is compelling. If the divine message communicated by angels is binding, carrying its own penalty for noncompliance, how much greater is the offense to despise or neglect the Son. At the start of chapter two, the writer presents the central theme, one to which he will often return. Since the Savior is more than an angel, it is extremely important that we listen to what He says.

This chapter also contains one of the most distinctive features in Hebrews. It alternates between doctrinal teaching and the practical expression of those truths. Thus, we are advised at the very beginning to be alert and attentive.

Here is a practical outline of chapter 2:

I. Pay attention! (2:1-4)
II. Jesus is one of us (2:5-9)
   A. Man's destiny (vv. 5-8b)
   B. Man's destiny frustrated (v. 8c)
   C. Man's destiny fulfilled in Jesus (v. 9)
III. Christ became a man (2:10-18)
   Here is why He became a man and not an angel:
   A. The kind of Savior we need (vv. 10-14a)
   B. The purpose of His death (vv. 14b-15)
   C. The perfect priest (vv. 16-18)

Lesson Development

I. PAY ATTENTION! (2:1-4)

Keep in clear focus this key truth: the Book of Hebrews was written to the Christian, not the sinner. Some of the key verses have been used effectively in evangelizing the non-Christian. Note 2:3 in this regard. However, the central message is to believers.

Read 2:1-4 in a modern language translation.

A. How important is the message of salvation? As you search for an answer, consider these related questions:

1. To what is our salvation compared?
2. Who announced our salvation?
3. How was our salvation confirmed?

B. In verse 1, the KJV translates the last phrase, "Lest at any time we should let them slip." The modern translators agree that the better translation is, "Lest we drift away from it" (2:1, NASB; also in NIV, RSV, and others).

1. Do you see any significant difference in these translations? If so, what is it?

2. What does it mean to "drift" in your Christian experience? How does a person drift? How do you keep from drifting? How do you stop?

C. Compare this phrase from verse 3, "How shall we escape if we ignore such a great salvation?" with verse 1, "Lest we drift away from it."

1. What does it have to say to the believer?
2. What is its message to the non-Christian?

D. In two short sentences, summarize what the writer was trying to say in verses 1-4.

II. JESUS IS ONE OF US (2:5-9)

1. Read this section from several modern versions.
2. Read Psalm 8 from the KJV and at least one modern language translation.

Psalm 8 is a hymn of praise to God and an ascription of high honor to man. There is no reference to the Messiah, none to Jesus. Man is exalted. He was created to have dominion.

But in reality man is frustrated by his inability, his failure. The basic Greek idea of God was detachment, the Christian revelation speaks of identity. This is the revolutionary truth: Christ is one of us!

A. Some versions translate verse 7, "You made him man for a little while lower than the angels" (NIV, margin). Others have it, "You made him a little lower than the angels."

1. Is there any important difference?
2. Which is more in line with Psalm 8?
3. Which do you prefer? Why?

B. What is man's destiny, as pictured here and in Psalm 8?

1. Has he lived up to his destiny?
2. Why has he fallen short?
3. How do each of us relate to that shortfall?
4. Which verse, or verses, highlight man's frustration?

C. How much hope for the future is contained in the phrase in verse 7, "Yet at present . . ."?

D. What did man fail to achieve over which Christ became the Conqueror?

E. Obviously, the writer did not see Christ's death as a tragic, cosmic blunder. What does it mean to you that "he suffered death, so that by the grace of God he might taste death for everyone" (v. 9)?

III. CHRIST BECAME A MAN (Read 2:10-18)

This section is an expansion of the triumphant truth of verse 9. Two key thoughts are established:

1. By His death Christ destroyed the one who holds the power of death (v. 14).

2. Thus, He became our merciful and faithful High Priest (vv. 17-18).

A. In what unusual way was the Son made perfect?

B. What does it mean for Christ to identify us as members of His family?

1. Select verses that support these two aspects of our family kinship with Christ.

_____ His participation in our human nature.

_____ Our participation in His holy nature.

2. What does the term *sanctify* (KJV) mean in verse 11?

3. Choose words that express how it feels to be a part of God's family.

C. Select the key phrases in verses 14-18 that highlight the ministry of Christ in relation to:

1. Our sin

2. Our temptations

IV. A SECOND LOOK

A. What is the most encouraging verse in chapter 2?

B. As a part of your spiritual preparation to face temptation, which verse or verses would it be helpful to memorize?

V. PRAYER TIME

A. As you review your relationship with Jesus Christ, for what are you most grateful? Put your gratitude in words—write out your prayer.

B. What are the circumstances and conditions that make you vulnerable to spiritual drifting? Decide what you will do this week to strengthen your life in these areas.

C. Picture one of the members of God's family that needs to be reassured that someone understands and cares for him. Plan one thing you can do for him this week.

VI. SOMETHING TO THINK ABOUT OR DO

To increase your awareness of the message of chapter 3, read about Moses, the great Old Testament leader. You will find these passages particularly helpful: Exod. 1:1—4:31; 12:1—20:21; 32:1—34:35.

3   He Is the Greatest

HEBREWS 3:1-19

"We can't all be heroes," said Will Rogers, "because someone has to sit on the curb and clap as they go by." We don't go for heroes much in our day. We have destroyed them either by gunfire or gossip, and there is a great emptiness in the land.

But it was not always that way. In nearly every culture in history men have lifted some people to special places of honor. These heroes have become their leaders, inspiring acts of devotion that made the impossible seem almost commonplace.

Because we look for ways to discredit those who rise above the common herd, we find it nearly impossible to understand how the Hebrew people revered Moses. He was their most respected leader. He spoke for God. An appeal to Moses settled all questions. He was greater than the patriarch Abraham, held in higher esteem than King David.

The revolutionary claim of the writer of the Book of Hebrews is that Jesus Christ stands so far above Moses that they cannot be compared. "This," says Richard Taylor, "was . . . the radical claim of authentic Christianity. If the Hebrew Christians really saw this, the almost hypnotic power of Moses over their minds would be broken forever. The Moses cult would hold no further fascination. Moses has fulfilled his task and passed away; the Son was not for a generation, but would rule the household of God forever" (BBC, vol. 10, pp. 43-44).

This is the thrust of chapter 3. Moses was an outstanding leader, greater than any other hero in Israel's history. But Christ stands alone. He is the greatest!

That fact, if accepted, has some tremendous implications, both doctrinal and practical. These are spotlighted in this chapter.

Because portions of chapter 3 are a bit difficult to understand, this outline will help us get everything in its proper place.

Introduction (3:1)
I. Christ is greater than Moses (3:2-6a)
    A. Because of His appointment (v. 2)
    B. Because of His nature (vv. 3-6a)
II. Warnings against disobedience (3:6b-19)
    The action of the Hebrew people in the wilderness is used to illustrate the danger of active unbelief.

Lesson Development

INTRODUCTION (3:1)

This verse contains these important truths:

1. The readers are identified as "holy brothers."
2. Jesus is called the apostle and the high priest whom we confess.

Only here in the New Testament is Jesus called an apostle. It is coupled with the key idea of Hebrews, Jesus is our High Priest. In brief, what the writer is saying is:

—an apostle is one who is sent forth: an envoy, ambassador, spokesman, one who represents another.

—a priest is the person who bridges the gap between God and man. To this key concept the writer will return many times.

I. CHRIST IS GREATER THAN MOSES (Read 3:2-6a)

A. Form groups with three people in each group. Each group will assign one of these letters to a person in that group: A, B, and C.

"C" will be the secretary for the threesome. His job will be to write down everything that is said. "A" and "B" are to represent impartial observers who were not a part of the inner circle.

"A" is to tell everything of a miraculous nature he can remember that happened while Moses was the leader of the Hebrew people. He is to imagine that he was an uninvolved bystander in Moses' time.

"B" is to recount the miracles of Jesus, likewise as an impartial observer.

After the participants have been identified, allow about 90 seconds for "A" and "B" to make notes. Then, on a starting signal, have "A" tell "B" and "C" everything he can recall about Moses. Each group is to do this simultaneously. Allow two minutes.

Now, have "B" tell "A" and "C" all he can about the miracle-working Christ. Allow about two minutes for this section also.

Bring the group back together. Have the "Cs" report on what "A" and "B" said in their threesome. On the basis of the reports discuss this question: "If you had been an impartial bystander, whose exploits would have seemed more dramatic, Moses' or Christ's?"

B. Do the reports from the groups justify the claims that Christ is greater than Moses? If not, on what does the writer base his claim?

C. Do you think that a similar argument could be made in our day between Jesus and any person in our national history?

D. In the Hebrew's comparison between Moses and Jesus, the Resurrection is not mentioned. Why?

E. The man who wrote the Book of Hebrews used different standards to judge people than his religious contemporaries used in their evaluation of Moses and Christ.

1. How did they differ?

2. Do those same differences occur today?

3. How do they affect your attitude toward Jesus Christ?

II. WARNINGS AGAINST DISOBEDIENCE (Read 3:6b-19)

A. In the last phrase of verse 6, the author moves from argument to application. He uses the picture of a house, its builder, and its servant. Discuss these questions:

1. What does the illustration of the house say to you about the nature of God and His hopes for the world?

2. What does the last phrase of this verse suggest about our security in Christ?

3. What practical instructions are given here?

B. The danger of rebellion (Read 3:7-19)

The writer now turns to the rebellion of the people in the wilderness. It was a rebellion both against Moses and the God he represented. Following an already established pattern in Hebrews, this new truth is seen against an Old Testament scripture: Ps. 95:7-11.

Read Psalm 95 from several translations.

It is important that you have a good understanding of this psalm, especially verses 7-11, because the rest of chapter 3 and all of chapter 4 are controlled by its message. Chapter 3 notes the warnings of the psalm, and chapter 4 proclaims the promises found there.

Spend a few minutes in quiet study of these related Old and New Testament passages. Use the information that you obtain from your study to discuss these questions with the group.

1. What is rebellion? its result? How can you identify it in yourself? in others? Is it easier to see in others? Are our perceptions always right—do we always see the truth in ourselves, and in others?

2. What are the two warnings identified in Ps. 95:7-11 and in verses 7 and 8 of Hebrews 3?

3. Satan's word is *tomorrow*. What impact does delay have on the truth contained in verses 12 and 13?

4. In what ways can Christians "encourage one another daily" as instructed in verse 13?

III. PRAYER TIME

1. Select a verse from chapter 3 through which the Lord is speaking to you. Write it in the space below.

2. Place in this space the initials of those members of the Body of Christ to whom you plan to give daily encouragement between now and the next session.

3. Write down the names of persons who live some distance from you that you will support daily with your prayers this week.

IV. SOMETHING TO THINK ABOUT OR DO

In lesson 4 we will study the writer's comparison between Joshua and Jesus. A careful reading of these scriptures in the Old Testament will provide a basic understanding of the great leader, Joshua: Num. 13:8, 16; 14:6-9; 27:18-23; Exod. 17:8-16; 24:13; 32:17; Josh. 1:1-18.

NOTES:

4   The Promise of Greater Rest

HEBREWS 4:1-13

Chapter 4 contains one of the more complicated passages in the Book of Hebrews. If you feel that way as you read, don't panic. Take those gems of truth that are more easily understood and work them into the fabric of your life. As you continue your study, many of the hidden passages will open up to you.

The truth of chapter 4 can be organized in this simple outline:
   I. The historical example (4:1-2)
   II. The rest of faith (4:3-11)
   III. The power of God's Word (4:12-13)

Now turn to chapter 4, a section that contains the exciting promise of God's presence in the lives of those who trust in Christ.

Lesson Development

I. THE HISTORICAL EXAMPLE (4:1-2)
Read Numbers 14:1-23.

1. In relation to the Old Testament background (Num. 14:1-23) what does this phrase mean, "Let us be careful that none of you be fallen short of it"? (v. 1). What are the modern implications? How does it speak to us?

2. An alternate, and acceptable, translation of the last phrase of verse 1 is, "Lest any of you should suppose himself to have come too late for it." If this translation is accepted as the message of this verse,
   a. How would it change its meaning?

    b. Would it be the source of greater faith in God, or less?

    c. Would it change anything you have planned to do in the next 30 days?

3. Verse 2 makes a comparison between the Israelites camped at Kadesh-barnea and the Hebrew Christians of the writer's day. What is the comparison?

4. What caused the Israelites to fall short when they faced their challenge? What advice is given in verse 2 that can help us in our Christian experience?

II. THE REST OF FAITH (Read 4:3-11)

A. This section contains one of the tougher sections of the book. Read it thoughtfully and in the space below, write in questions about anything you do not understand.

In your group meeting, share these questions and answers. Do not spend more than 10 minutes discussing them at this time. However, keep them in mind during this, and later sessions. Many answers will come to you as you work your way through the rest of the book.

Even though we may not be able to completely follow the complicated argument, the message of the whole section is clear: If the promise of God to His people had been fulfilled when they entered Canaan under Joshua's guidance, the Psalmist would not have needed to write the 95th psalm. If the psalm-singers had found the answer, the writer to the Hebrews would not be speaking of a further fulfillment: "Therefore, since the promise of entering his rest still stands, let us be careful that none of you be found to have fallen short of it" (v. 1). And again, "There remains, then, a Sabbath-rest for the people of God" (v. 9).

"The rest that is promised," writes W. T. Purkiser, "is therefore a rest for the people of God; it is a rest of faith; it is entering a state compared to God's own rest. Gone are the ceaseless strivings for perfection in human endeavor. Gone are the struggles with a self against itself, the double-mindedness of a carnal heart. This is not the rest of inactivity; it is the rest of equilib-rium" (BBE, vol. 11, pp. 42-43).

F. B. Meyer adds, it is a "perfect equilibrium between the outgoings and the incomings of the life; to a contented heart; to a peace that passeth all understanding; to the repose of the will in the will of God; and to the calm of the depths of the nature which are undisturbed by the hurricanes which sweep the surface, and urge forward the mighty waves" (BBE, vol. 11, p. 43).

B. The exciting message of verse 9 is that God's promise is still valid. People may have failed to take advantage of the promise in their day, but that did not destroy the promise.

1. What does the writer mean by the phrase, "a Sabbath-rest for the people of God"?

2. Review verses 1-11:
   a. What attitudes should a person take toward the promise?

   b. How can you enter into this rest?

C. Read verse 11 again. Discuss these questions: How much responsi-bility does a person have for the impact of his example on someone else? Is a person responsible for his influence? How much should he adjust his life in relation to others? Where is the boundary line between freedom and responsibility?

D. Note the similarity between verse 1 and verse 11.

Verse 11 is a common feature in Hebrews, a carefully constructed transition. It serves as a conclusion to the early part of the chapter, and an open door to verses 12 and 13. The central idea is that the ancients were not trifling with the advice of a fellow Hebrew, Moses or Joshua. They were rejecting the Word of God.

III. THE POWER OF GOD'S WORD (Read 4:12-13)

A casual reading of this chapter might lead one to the conclusion that verses 12 and 13 are irrelevant to the discussion. Careful examination, how-ever, reveals that they form a powerful conclusion to this section.

A. What do these verses have to say about the Word of God? When you consider God's Word as described here, what do you think about? List some key words that describe your feelings:

B. How much of our life, attitude, and action can be hidden from God? Do you live each day as if you really believed the answer the Bible gives to this question?

IV. PRAYER TIME

A. In a column on the left below, list any difficulties or problems that disturb your spiritual rest. Opposite each item listed, write in anything you can do or are doing to reach a more restful state in relation to these challenges.

B. Share with your Bible study partners any special needs you wish them to pray about this week. Write their requests in the space below, and pray each day for them.

V. SOMETHING TO THINK ABOUT OR DO

In your personal prayer time and Bible study this week, search for promises or guidance that will help you find rest for the needs listed in section IV.

5   Jesus Qualifies to Be Our High Priest

HEBREWS 4:14—5:10

The Book of Hebrews is a carefully reasoned argument. In a logical manner that would have been easily understood by first-century Hebrew Christians, Christ is shown to be our Savior because He is our great High Priest.

The first part of this section, 4:14-16, has been called "The Transitional Passage" by Wiley in *The Epistle to the Hebrews* (p. 160). In the first four chapters the writer has proclaimed that Jesus Christ is superior to any part of and all of the Old Testament. Our Lord has been declared to be greater than the angels, God's servants; superior to Moses, God's representative; above and beyond Joshua, the man who led Israel into Canaan.

We note a shift in mood at this point in the book. In 4:12-13 men stand naked before the all-seeing, all-powerful God. "Everything is uncovered and laid bare before the eyes of him to whom we must give account" (v. 13).

But that is not the end of the story. "We have a great high priest" (v. 14). "From here on the vocabulary stresses new words. Sympathy, confidence, grace, mercy, help—these give a new tone to the passage, and become the big words in our experience" (J. C. Macaulay, quoted in BBE, vol. 11, p. 45).

Jesus Christ is our Savior because He is our High Priest. That fact dominates the remainder of the book. The author will return to it on many occasions, each time holding up a different aspect for wonder and praise. Here at the beginning of this new mood we are encouraged to see how Jesus Christ meets all the qualifications to be our High Priest.

In order to appreciate more fully verses 14-16 of chapter 4, our study will begin in chapter 5. Then, we will return to what many believe is the high point in the Book of Hebrews.

This brief outline will help open up the passage:

    I. A word about the high priest (5:1-4)

    II. Christ's appointment as High Priest (5:5-6)

    III. Christ's humanity (5:7-9)

    IV. Jesus, our Great High Priest (4:14-16)

Lesson Development

I. A WORD ABOUT THE HIGH PRIEST (Read 5:1-4)

A. These verses identify six requirements for the office of high priest. To aid you in your search, the verses where they can be found are identified. In your group study, join with the person sitting next to you and find the six qualifications. Write them in the proper places.

    1. v. 1—
    2. v. 1—
    3. v. 1—
    4. v. 2—
    5. v. 3—
    6. v. 4—

B. After all of the members of the group have had a chance to complete the list, share your findings with the entire group.

C. Select the two or three qualifications that you think are the most important.

II. CHRIST'S APPOINTMENT AS HIGH PRIEST (Read 5:5-6)

A. For a quick review of the beginnings of the high priesthood in the Old Testament, turn to

    1. Exod. 28:1-5, where Aaron and his sons are selected, by God;

    2. Num. 20:22-29, where the high priesthood is transferred to Eleazar (El-ee-AY-zar) at Aaron's death.

B. Christ's appointment as our High Priest. Circle the correct answer: True or False.

T F 1. Christ was selected to be our High Priest because He was a descendant of Aaron.

T F 2. Christ nominated himself for the priesthood.

T F 3. Christ was chosen by the same person who selected Aaron to be the high priest.

T F 4. The high priesthood of Christ is to be completely different from Aaron's.

What do your answers tell you about the relative value of Christ's priesthood as compared with Aaron's?

In this section, Christ is compared to Melchizedek (Mel-KIZ-e-dek, vv. 6, 10). Since this is the major thrust of chapter 7, we will defer our study of this interesting Old Testament spiritual leader until we get to lesson 7.

III. CHRIST'S HUMANITY (5:7-9)

Read this section from several modern language translations.

A. List the things in these verses that do not seem to be godlike—things you would not expect an all-powerful God to do.

B. What phrase, or part of a verse, explains why Christ's actions are more human than divine?

C. Clearly the writer is saying that Christ had to become human to become our Savior. Why do you think this was necessary? Do you like the idea?

D. Can you remember some events in the earthly life of our Lord that illustrate the portrait of Christ given in verses 7-9?

IV. JESUS, OUR GREAT HIGH PRIEST
   (Turn back and read 4:14-16)

A. In your group study, select someone to read this section aloud from a modern language translation. Close your eyes and concentrate on the message of these verses as you hear them. When the reading has been completed, write down your immediate reaction.

B. What do these verses tell us about Christ?
   1. As a person?
   2. As our High Priest?

C. What is the one thing that sets Christ off from all other members of the human race (note v. 15)? In the context of our study section, how important is this distinction?

D. Because Christ is our great High Priest, what are we encouraged to do? If you took verse 16 seriously, would it make any difference in your relationship with God and with people?

V. PRAYER TIME

The translation of the New Testament by Charles Williams gives special attention to the tenses of the verbs in the original Greek. He translates verse 16 in the present tense, which indicates a continuing action: "So let us continue coming with courage to the throne of God's unmerited favor to obtain His mercy and to find His spiritual strength to help us when we need it."

Center your faith on this verse as you share in prayer. Take as your promise for the week the invitation to "continue coming with courage."

VI. SOMETHING TO THINK ABOUT OR DO

Copy 4:14-16 from your favorite translation on a 3 x 5 card. Carry it with you this week. Refer to it often. Before the week is over you may decide to memorize it.

6

Keep on Growing

HEBREWS 5:11—6:20

We have now come to the point where we will explore the reason the Book of Hebrews was written. Earlier in chapter 5, we had a brief glimpse of this magnificent truth, but it will be the central theme of chapters 7—10: Jesus is our Savior because He is our great High Priest.

The priestly concept is not a familiar one to us, but it has important truths that show us Christ's ministry. So if at some point along the way everything is not immediately clear, let's try to dig a little deeper. The effort will be rewarding.

But before we cross the threshold to our study of the central truth of Hebrews, we pause for the following interlude. It is time to ask the Lord to help us take a careful look at the depth of our devotion to Him and His kingdom.

An outline of 5:11—6:20

   I. A refusal to grow up (5:11-14)

   II. The importance of growth (6:1-3)

   III. Spiritual death (6:4-8)

   IV. But there is still hope (6:9-20)

      A. Hebrew Christians are still loved by God (vv. 9-15)

         1. The need for diligence (vv. 11-12)

         2. The example of Abraham (vv. 13-15)

      B. God keeps His promises (vv. 16-20)

         1. His oath (vv. 16-17)

         2. Our hope (vv. 18-20)

Lesson Development

I. A REFUSAL TO GROW UP (Read 5:11-14)

A. Why, do you suppose, the writer inserts these warnings against failure to grow and backsliding?

B. Many Bible scholars, commenting on this section, mention a willful rejection rather than a careless fumbling with holy things. (See 10:26-27 for a clear statement of this truth.) Do you see any support for this position as you read these verses?

C. What clues are given in verses 11-14 that help us understand the early Christians' spiritual instability?

D. Do the same problems exist today? How can a person combat the temptation to become dull and lazy in his Christian experience?

E. What emphasis on personal discipline is given in 5:14? How important do you think discipline is for Christian growth?

II. THE IMPORTANCE OF GROWTH (Read 6:1-3)

A. A threefold foundation of our life in Christ is identified in verses 1-2.
1. Personal salvation
   a. "repentance from acts that lead to death"
   b. "faith in God"
2. Church ritual
   a. "instruction about baptisms"
   b. "laying on of hands"
3. End-of-time events
   a. "the resurrection of the dead"
   b. "eternal judgment"

B. In view of this exhortation and these guidelines for growth, evaluate your own progress in the Christian life.

C. The instruction is to "leave the elementary teachings of Jesus and go on to maturity." What do you think it means to leave these teachings?

To forget or ignore them? Yes_____ No_____
To accept them as true? Yes_____ No_____
To consider them as foundation truths but not all of God's truth?
Yes_____ No_____

D. Have a brainstorming session in your Bible study group. In rapid-fire fashion list the qualities a mature Christian possesses. Write them in the space below. In personal preparation, list some qualities that you expect in mature Christians.

Take a few quiet moments to reflect on these qualities. In all honesty, how many of them do you find in your own life? Give yourself credit for the growth you are making. Be willing to recognize those areas where you need to ask God to help you improve.

Use these symbols in front of the qualities on the list, to reflect your present achievement and future hope.

⟋ —I am making good progress here

⊖ —stalemated on this one

⊙ —just beginning to understand

⌐ —recently took a big step

⟍ —losing ground in relation to this aspect of Christian maturity

! —need lots of help here

III. SPIRITUAL DEATH (Read 6:4-8)

Chapter 10, verses 19-39 are an additional resource for this section.

A. The writer's reluctance to give further light in 5:11 goes beyond man's limited mental capabilities. Clearly we are told that there are some mysteries of the faith that can be understood only by those who believe in and devotedly follow the Lord Jesus Christ.

There are, also, some awesome practical implications that flow from these facts. The writer projects the tragic possibility of rejecting Christ. Eternal destinies are involved. It is possible, he asserts, to become so calloused in our relationship with the Lord that we will be cut off forever from Him.

Many people have tried to drain these frightening words in 6:4-8 of their terror. But to deny their true message would be to rewrite the Holy Word. This we must not do. But, at the same time, we need to understand exactly what is meant by these ominous words. "This passage," writes F. B. Meyer in *The Way into the Holiest*, "has nothing to do with those who fear lest it condemns them. The presence of anxiety, like the cry which betrayed the real mother in the days of Solomon, establishes beyond a doubt that you are not one that has fallen away beyond the possibility of renewal to repentance" (p. 81).

B. Many Bible translators note that the Greek participle in verse 6 is in the present tense. It is therefore accurate to translate the sentence "It is impossible for those who have been enlightened . . . if they fall away, to be brought back to repentance, *while** to their loss they are crucifying the Son of God all over again . . ."

In what significant way does this translation change the meaning of these verses? Is it more understandable? More helpful?

C. Discuss ways Christians can help each other to keep from becoming calloused to the point of totally rejecting Christ.

IV. BUT THERE IS STILL HOPE (6:9-20)

A. Read aloud from a modern language translation.

B. A significant change of mood occurs at verse 9. Only here in the book does the writer address his readers as "dear friends." Quickly he moves to establish hope lest they should have become discouraged.

C. List below the reasons given in these verses that bring hope and encouragement to the believers. Which one is most meaningful to you?

V. PRAYER TIME

A. Select a person, or family, who once were active in your church, but are now not involved. Pray for them now and during the week.

B. Pray that the Lord will send a spirit of revival to your church.

VI. SOMETHING TO THINK ABOUT OR DO

In preparation for lesson 7, read Gen. 14:17-20; Psalm 110.

(*NIV margin.)

7   Better than the Best

HEBREWS 7:1-28

In our study this week we are to examine chapters 7 and 8. First, read these two chapters through and then write below one sentence stating what seems to you to be the author's most important concern.

William Barclay, in *The Letter to the Hebrews,* helps us understand these chapters when he writes, the Hebrew "starts with the basic idea that *religion is access to God.*" In order for man to reach God, two things were created: the Law and the priesthood.

"The basic idea of the law is that so long as a man faithfully and obediently observes the commandments of the law, he is in a position of friendship with God, and the door to God's presence is open to him" (p. 68).

The priest was "a man whose function it was to build a bridge between men and God. How? By means of the sacrificial system" (p. 68).

In actual practice, however, the sacrifices could not bring a man to the place where he could be victorious over sin. They regularly highlighted his failure. The old system was inadequate. A new system, a new covenant, a new priesthood was needed. Jesus Christ became that great High Priest and thus ushered in a new covenant bringing not only forgiveness, but the power to change men's lives so they could live above sin. (Read Barclay's *The Letter to the Hebrews,* pp. 68 ff.)

The writer to the Hebrews felt it necessary to shatter any remaining dependence on Judaism. To do that he had to convince these Hebrew Christians of three things:

1. The priesthood of Christ completely destroys and displaces the whole structure of the Jewish priesthood and Temple worship.

2. Jesus, in His priesthood, inaugurated a new covenant between God and His people, making the old covenant obsolete.

3. The person and work of Christ are final, and cancel all other ways to reach God. Having come to know Christ as Savior and Lord, Christians dare not return to their former faith. (For the full discussion see BBC, vol. 10, pp. 78-80.)

Chapter 8 continues and elaborates on the superior priesthood and ministry of Christ. This chapter is helpful also as introductory reading for the next two lessons. Our concentration, however, in this lesson is on chapter 7. The following outline from the *Beacon Bible Commentary* will help us to organize our study.

I. The order of Melchizedek (7:1-10)
   A. A review of Genesis 14:18-20 (vv. 1-2a)
   B. The pattern of his priesthood (vv. 2b-3)
   C. The greatness of his priesthood (vv. 4-10)

II. The old order displaced by the new (7:11-22)
   A. The impotence of the Levitical order (v. 11)
   B. The annulment of the Mosaic Law (vv. 12-19)
   C. The inauguration of a "better" testament (vv. 20-22)
      (Chapter 8 provides excellent additional background reading for this section.)

III. A perfect salvation in a perfected Savior (7:23-28)
   A. A perfected power to save (vv. 23-25)
   B. A perfected Person who saves (vv. 26-28)

Lesson Development

I. THE ORDER OF MELCHIZEDEK (7:1-10; Gen. 14:18-20; Ps. 110:4)

In your study time form small groups with two or three in each. Read the scripture passages listed above. Place a check (✔) in front of the correct answer of each of these multiple-choice questions. When everyone has completed the study, compare your answers.

1. Melchizedek was
   a. a friend of Abraham
   b. the king of Salem
   c. a tribal chief who controlled a toll road

2. This man who collected the tithe from Abraham was
   a. a member of the tribe of Levi
   b. the leader of the tribe of Judah
   c. a part of some unknown family

3. The phrase "without beginning of days or end of life" means that
   a. Melchizedek did not die but went to heaven like Enoch.
   b. His ancestry had nothing to do with his priesthood.
   c. He lost his copy of the family tree.

II. THE OLD ORDER DISPLACED BY THE NEW

Barclay suggests these four key ideas that dominate the remainder of chapter 7:

1. Jesus is the High Priest, whose priesthood depends not on any genealogy, but on himself and himself alone.

2. Jesus is the High Priest who lives forever and never dies.

3. Jesus is the High Priest who himself is sinless and never needs to offer any sacrifice for His own sin.

4. Jesus is the High Priest who in the offering of himself made the perfect sacrifice. No more does sacrifice need to be made every day. Once and for all the sacrifice has been made which opens the way to God (Barclay, *Letter to the Hebrews*, p. 74).

A. Working as a group, search verses 11-28, looking for scriptural support for each of the ideas listed above. In the space provided, write below each statement the references that support it.

B. Discuss these questions:
1. How did a person qualify to become a priest in Old Testament times?
2. How did Christ's appointment to the priesthood differ from that of Old Testament priests?
3. How is Christ's priesthood better than the old order? Note especially verses 18-19, 23-25.

III. A PERFECT SALVATION IN A PERFECTED SAVIOR

A. Read 7:25 in several translations.
1. What feelings do you have when you read it, or hear it read?
2. Select the key words in this verse.

B. A portion of this verse can be correctly translated two different ways:
—"save completely"
—"save forever" (NASB)
1. What are the implications of each translation?
2. What encouragement does each add to your faith in Christ?
3. Which do you need to hear most clearly right now?

IV. PRAYER TIME

Begin your prayer time with a period of guided prayer. Have all close their books and sit quietly with closed eyes. As the leader guides you, pray silently for each of these things in order:

—thank the Lord for forgiveness for sin.

—reaffirm your decision to fully commit everything in your life to Him.

—ask the Lord to help you understand any area in your life where you need to grow more like Christ.

—give to the Lord the concern that is causing you the greatest anxiety at this moment.

—pray for the person sitting to your right—then, for the person on your left.

At an appropriate time the leader, or someone he selects, should pray aloud for the group.

V. SOMETHING TO THINK ABOUT OR DO

In the Bible, blood represented life. Lesson 8, Hebrews 9:11-28, will consider the blood of Jesus Christ as it relates to our salvation. The following verses will contribute to your understanding of this important theme: Lev. 17:10-14; 1 Cor. 10:16; 1 Pet. 1:2, 19; 1 John 1:7; Rev. 12:11.

8   The Covenant Bond

HEBREWS 9:1-28

We have now come to the climax of the writer's argument. It is the point toward which he has been moving since his first words, "In the past God spoke to our forefathers . . . but in these last days he has spoken to us by his Son" (1:1-2). The section from 9:11—10:18 is the core of the Book of Hebrews. Christ has been shown to be superior to the Old Testament, both its ritual and its heroes. Now the author will present arguments designed to demonstrate that our Lord is the fulfillment of the Levitical sacrificial system.

This lesson, verses 11-28, probes the meaning of the words, "without the shedding of blood there is no forgiveness" (9:22).

But we have a communications problem. Hebrews rests on the Old Testament, especially requiring an understanding of the Tabernacle and the worship God ordained in it. We must study the historical background before we can appreciate the symbolism.

The difficulty we face is similar to the problem that occurs when a football addict tries to explain the intricacies of the game to his athletically uninformed wife. He uses terms like: trap-block, splitting the seam, zone coverage, off-tackle slant, and moving pocket. She is as mystified as he is when she talks about a French seam on her dress or the purl stitch she uses while knitting. Each is using the language of the insider.

To understand Hebrews we must move inside through a careful study of some key Old Testament passages. They will provide the background for understanding the exciting truth presented here.

Lesson Development

I. BASIC BACKGROUND (9:1-10)

Stay with these 10 verses until you have a pretty good idea what they mean. You cannot fully understand this section until you fix in your mind the picture of ancient Hebrew worship.

Among the alternatives you could use in studying the Old Testament are these:

1. Private study at home between Bible study sessions as the basis of mutual sharing.

2. Assignment of specific homework to each individual, asking for a report to the group.

3. Divide the group into committees of two or three, and let each explore a part, or parts, of the Old Testament suggested. Have each committee report their findings to the group.

The following paragraphs list the most helpful passages relating to the Tabernacle, its furniture and furnishings, and the ritual of the great Day of Atonement. A diagram of the Tabernacle is shown on page 46.

The blood of the covenant (Exod. 24:5-8)

Furniture for the Tabernacle
    Ark of the Covenant (Exod. 25:10-22)
    The Table of Shewbread (Exod. 25:23-30)
    Lampstand (Exod. 25:31-40)

Construction of the Tabernacle (Exod. 26:1-37)
    Altar of burnt offering (Exod. 27:1-8)
    Courtyard (Exod. 27:9-19)
    Oil for lampstands (Exod. 27:20-21)

Priestly garments (Exod. 28:1-43; esp. v. 4)
    Ephod (Exod. 28:6-14)
    Breastpiece (Exod. 28:15-30)
    Other garments (Exod. 28:31-43)

Consecration of the Priests (Exod. 29:1-46)

Altar of Incense (Exod. 30:1-10)
Atonement money (Exod. 30:11-16)
Basin for washing (Exod. 30:17-21)
Anointing Oil (Exod. 30:22-33)
Incense (Exod. 30:34-38)

(The actual construction of the Tabernacle is reported in Exodus 35—40.)

The Day of Atonement (Leviticus 16:1-34)

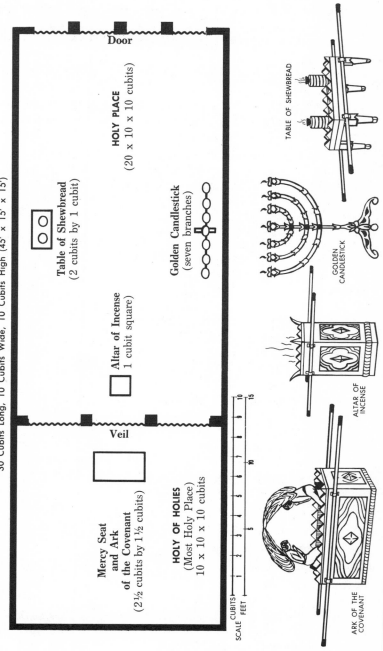

PLAN OF THE TABERNACLE IN THE WILDERNESS
30 Cubits Long, 10 Cubits Wide, 10 Cubits High (45' x 15' x 15')

Door

HOLY PLACE
(20 x 10 x 10 cubits)

Table of Shewbread
(2 cubits by 1 cubit)

Altar of Incense
1 cubit square

Golden Candlestick
(seven branches)

Veil

**Mercy Seat
and Ark
of the Covenant**
(2½ cubits by 1½ cubits)

HOLY OF HOLIES
(Most Holy Place)
10 x 10 x 10 cubits

SCALE
CUBITS
FEET

TABLE OF SHEWBREAD

GOLDEN
CANDLESTICK

ALTAR OF
INCENSE

ARK OF THE
COVENANT

II. SUMMARY (9:11-28)

On the basis of your Old Testament study, complete the following charts.

A. Note the points of contrast between the old system and Christ; use verses 11-14 as your resource.

Old System	Jesus Christ
1. Earthly Tabernacle	
2. Blood of goats and calves	
3. Entered holy of holies every year	
4. Outwardly clean	
5. Sacrifices were helpless victims	
6. Ritual forgiveness	

B. Three great appearances of Christ are mentioned in verses 23-28.

	Verse	For what purpose
1. In the past		
2. In the present		
3. In the future		

Compare these verses with the atonement ritual in Leviticus 16.

III. APPLICATION

Read 9:11-28 in your favorite Bible. Select a verse that best fits each of the categories below. Write it in the appropriate space. Be prepared to share the reason you selected it.

A. The most helpful

B. The most demanding

C. The one first-century Hebrew Christians would have found most difficult to understand.

D. The one I find most difficult to understand.

My attitude toward chapter 9 before we began this study was (underline one):
—confusion
—excitement
—boredom

— _____

Now my attitude is:
—still confused
—somewhat greater understanding
—encouraged

— _____

IV. PRAYER TIME

A. Share, as people may be willing, your personal testimonies. Give praise to the Lord for the forgiveness you are now experiencing.

B. Accept prayer requests for persons who need to make a decision to follow Jesus Christ.

C. Pray also for the current needs of those in your Bible study group.

V. SOMETHING TO THINK ABOUT OR DO

Read chapters 9 and 10 each day this week. Read from a variety of translations if they are available.

9   Christ's Perfect Sacrifice

HEBREWS 10:1-25

This is sacred territory, the climactic portion of the inspired writer's reasoned discussion on the meaning and power of Christ's death on the Cross. It is here that final conclusions are presented along with the dramatic possibilities in store for every Christian.

There are distinct shifts in mood and emphasis in this section. The first is at Hebrews 10:1 which reveals a significant change from chapter 9. As Richard Taylor notes in vol. 10 of *Beacon Bible Commentary,* the emphasis in chapter 9 is on the preparation of earthly places of worship. The writer describes how our Lord ratifies the new testament and consecrates the new spiritual order with His blood. Christ is the fulfillment of the requirements of Old Testament ceremonial religion. He is the perfect fulfillment of the ancient rituals.

Now, our author advances to an exciting new level in his thinking. Our Lord's precious blood not only met all the demands of the Law, but also opened up "a new and living way" (v. 20). The redemption Christ purchased on the Cross is much more than a legal transaction. The veil has been torn apart; the restrictions have been removed. We can enter into the presence of a holy God—without fear! This includes both "a justification which brings peace and a sanctification (both 'initial' and 'entire') which makes clean" (BBC, vol. 10, p. 116).

The essence of the argument in 10:1-18 is that the ceremonial law required continual sacrifice. By the very fact of its repetition, it signalled that the sacrifices were inadequate. Every Day of Atonement was a fresh reminder of man's inability to rise above sin. But we are told, Christ "takes away the first in order to establish the second. By this will we have been sanctified through the offering of the body of Jesus Christ once for all." And again, "For by one offering He has perfected for all time those who are sanctified" (vv. 9-10, 14, NASB). "The supreme act of Jesus to the Father's will both satisfies the law and sanctifies the believer" (BBE, vol. 11, p. 78).

Here is a simple outline of 10:1-25.

I. A final argument (10:1-18)
   A. Repeated animal sacrifices reveal their inadequacy (vv. 1-4)
   B. The new and living way in Christ (vv. 5-10)
   C. The meaning and power of Christ's death (vv. 11-18)
      10:18—the end of the argument in Hebrews
      10:19—the beginning of the exhortations which continue to the end of the book
II. Important instructions (10:19-25)
   A. Boldness to enter the holiest place (vv. 19-22)
   B. Three significant exhortations (vv. 23-25)

Lesson Development

I. A SECOND LOOK AT CHAPTER 9

There are three key ideas in chapter 9 that form the foundation for the new truth in chapter 10 (BBC). Review chapter 9 to find the verse, or verses, that reveal each truth. Write their location in the space in front of each statement.

Verse

_____ 1. We must not lose sight of our goal: free access into the presence of a holy God.

_____ 2. Only the blood of Jesus Christ can cleanse our hearts, qualifying us to enter His presence.

_____ 3. Christ's sacrifice for our sins was complete—once for all: for all time, for all people, for all our sin.

II. A FINAL ARGUMENT (10:1-18)

A. Repeated animal sacrifices reveal their inadequacy (Read 10:1-4)

1. Spend a short period of time reviewing the ritual the high priest performed on the Day of Atonement each year.

2. Circle any of the following words that you think represent how the high priest felt when he entered the holy of holies on the Day of Atonement. Add any words you wish. Discuss your selections with the group.

fear	anger	inadequacy	hope
anxiety	joy	unimportance	trust in God
peace	love	price	vulnerability
anticipation	reluctance	sinfulness	guilt
_____	_____	_____	_____

Do you find any of these implied in verses 1-4?

3. If the high priest could have had the assurance that his prayers would be answered, what would he have asked God when he stood before the mercy seat in the holy of holies?

B. The new and living way in Christ (Read 10:5-10)

1. William Barclay, in *The Letter to the Hebrews*, notes that the central truth here is, "The only sacrifice God wants from man is obedience . . . but human nature being what it is, it was fatally easy for the idea of sacrifice to be thought of as a way of buying the forgiveness of God" (p. 127).

List the ways people in our day appear to be trying to appease God or purchase salvation through what they do for God, or give to Him.

2. If it is true, as the Old Testament prophets often proclaimed, that obedience is the only acceptable sacrifice, then it becomes clear why Christ's sacrifice could be perfect and final. He alone, of all men, was able to give full and complete obedience to the Father's will. (For an inspiring analysis of this thought, see Barclay's *The Letter to the Hebrews*, pp. 127-29).

Pause for a quiet moment of meditation and personal spiritual inspection. Ask yourself these questions.

   a. Have I given everything to Jesus Christ: my past, present, and future—all I own and all I love?

   b. Is there anything I earlier placed on the altar of commitment that I have removed and placed under my control rather than leaving it under His control?

   c. Is the Lord showing me anything right at this moment, that He wants me to give to Him?

   d. Am I now experiencing forgiveness of sins, and the presence of the Holy Spirit in my life in sanctifying power? Read 10:10; 13:11-14.

III. IMPORTANT INSTRUCTIONS (Read 10:19-25)

The time for mere logic is past. The writer now demands action—actions in the light of verse 25, "All the more as you see the Day [the second coming of Christ] approaching."

A. Boldness to enter the holiest place (10:19-22). Read this section aloud from a modern language translation.

1. What is the Old Testament background to these verses? (See 9:6-7.)

2. What emotions do you feel as the passage is being read?

3. If you really took these instructions seriously, what would you do?

B. Three significant exhortations (10:23-25). List them below.

1. *(a)* v. 23

   (b) v. 24

   (c) v. 25

2. React to this sentence: "The man who does not worship God at a particular time and at a particular place, ceases in the end to worship God anywhere" (Norman Snaith in BBE, vol. 11, p. 83).

IV. PRAYER TIME

1. Use the four questions above under "The new and living way in Christ" as the basis of your praying together.

2. Praise the Lord for complete victory in your life.

V. SOMETHING TO THINK ABOUT OR DO

Read 10:35—11:38 several times between now and the next Bible study session. Why did the author include this section right at this place in his book?

10   The Way of Faith

HEBREWS 10:26—11:38

Like a bolt of lightning our author changes the mood once again. We have just been encouraged to enter boldly into the most holy place by the blood of Jesus. We have been advised to prepare ourselves and assist our friends in preparation for the second coming of Christ.

Now, without warning, we are told, "If we deliberately keep on sinning after we have received the knowledge of the truth, no sacrifice for sins is left" (10:26). Sublime promise and terrifying judgment come in close-order formation.

There are few places in the Bible where the fate of the unrepentant backslider is portrayed in such terrifying terms as here, and in 5:11—6:8. You may want to review lesson 6 before you proceed, especially that portion relating to backsliding and apostasy.

What were the conditions that caused the writer to send these stern but faithful warnings to those who had once known Christ but had turned back to their old life?

Barclay suggests in his exposition on 10:32-39, that these Christians had experienced persecution without wavering. As the ancient hymn puts it, their faith did "not shrink, tho' pressed by every foe," nor did it "tremble on the brink of any earthly woe." Yet, when things become easier they relaxed in their devotion to Christ with tragic results. There are some indications that this may have been the historic situation. If so, we can readily identify with it. It speaks to our age.

Here is a simple outline of the passage we are going to study together:

I. The alternatives to faith (10:26-39)
  A. Devotion or disaster (vv. 26-31)
  B. Remember past steadfastness (vv. 32-34)
  C. The faith-way is not optional (vv. 35-39)
II. The heritage of faith (11:1-40)

Building a Foundation

With some minor variations, the outline below is taken from F. B. Meyer (p. 132). Search for scripture verse(s) that teach the truth in each statement.

Verse(s)

    1. Note the author's threefold conclusion
_____   a. We may enter the holiest by the blood of Jesus.
_____   b. Jesus has inaugurated a new and living way.
_____   c. We have a Great High Priest.

    2. Review the threefold exhortation
_____   a. Let us draw near.
_____   b. Let us hold fast.
_____   c. Let us consider one another.

    3. Observe the threefold exhortation
_____   a. Go forward—otherwise penalty.
_____   b. Go forward—otherwise past efforts nullified.
_____   c. Go forward—the Lord is at hand.

Using this as our foundation, let us look for the reasons why the writer concludes his Epistle with a strong message on faith.

Lesson Development

I. THE ALTERNATIVES TO FAITH (10:26-39)

A. Devotion or disaster (10:26-31)

Compare these verses with 5:11—6:8, which you studied in lesson 6. Do you see any significant difference between these two sections? What three reasons are given indicating that the renegade Christian deserves such terrible judgment? What is said about the exclusiveness of the Christian religion?

B. Remember past steadfastness (10:32-34)

Once again, the mood changes abruptly from the possibility of awesome judgment to a tender, personal appeal. He asks his readers to compare the days of persecution when their devotion was at its peak with their current spiritual condition.

1. Form groups of three or four. Let your imagination loose to roam freely. Who do you think they were? What kind of people were they? What was the reason this letter was written? What was their spiritual state?

Put together a composite picture of the first readers of this epistle. Share your conclusions with the entire group.

2. There are subtle indications in this section that these first-century Hebrew Christians had drifted away from the intensity of devotion they had known at the beginning. Can you find these indications in these verses? How does our generation compare in this regard? How do you rate yourself?

C. The faith-way is not optional (10:35-39)

The writer's logic is simple. In view of the awful consequences of apostasy and the great things God has done in the past, now is not the time to quit. He concludes with a great affirmation, "But we are not of those who shrink back and are destroyed, but of those who believe and are saved" (v. 39).

1. What is your reaction to this sentence, "Faith is not belief in spite of evidence; it is life in scorn of consequence" (Kirsopp Lake, quoted in BBE, vol. 11, p. 88)?

2. Remember that in the original there were no chapter and verse divisions. The letter did not have an artificial interruption here. In what ways is our understanding of chapter 11 affected by using 10:35-39 as an introduction?

II. THE HERITAGE OF FAITH (11:1-40)

Without a doubt this is the best-known section of the Book of Hebrews. It deserves its acclaim. The intent of this study is to help us understand it better and to see that it is a vital part of the whole.

Because of its significance to our study, the next lesson will be devoted to an exploration of this faith chapter. As we read through this chapter before the next session, we will see that the writer is emphasizing the fact that the way of faith is not something new. The rich heritage of God's people is due to the faith-way their forefathers took in the centuries past.

III. PRAYER TIME

1. Spend some time in quiet meditation asking the Lord to identify any place in your spiritual life where you are "drifting."

2. Share your prayer requests with the group.

3. Pray for each one, and others in your acquaintance, who need to experience spiritual renewal.

IV. SOMETHING TO THINK ABOUT OR DO

Read chapter 11 several times this week, asking the Holy Spirit to give you a greater understanding of its truths and their application to your life.

NOTES:

11   Examples of Faithful Living

HEBREWS 11:1-40

There is a special kind of reverence that the devout give to sacred places. Both the wordless communication of the body and the spoken language reflect this attitude. People walk and talk softly. Holy places are entered with adoration.

Hebrews 11 has been given that kind of veneration by Christians. When we read through these verses it is as though we are walking in a gallery of heroes, a Hebrew Hall of Fame.

Yet, in the midst of the tour, certain questions keep recurring. Why did the author include these examples of faithful living? Why was their record inserted here? Keep these questions before you as you study this chapter. There is no single, simple answer, but an awareness of the reasons will enhance your understanding of this great chapter.

These verses provide a description of faith rather than a formal definition. This outline by Harvey E. Finley will give the big picture.

  I. Faith defined (11:1-3)
    A. Faith is the key to divine approval (v. 2)
    B. Faith, alone, brings understanding of creation (v. 3)
  II. Faith illustrated (11:4-12, 17-38)
    A. Abel—a more acceptable sacrifice (v. 4)
    B. Enoch—did not see death (vv. 5-6)
    C. Noah—constructed ark and inherited righteousness (v. 7)
    D. Abraham—obeyed God (vv. 8-12, 17-18)
    E. Isaac—promised blessings (v. 20)
    F. Jacob—blessed sons of Joseph (v. 21)
    G. Joseph—foresaw the Exodus (v. 22)
    H. Moses—chose to serve Jehovah (vv. 23-28)
    I. Many others—suffered and endured to the glory of God (vv. 29-38)
  III. By faith and yet short of the promise (11:13-16, 39-40)
    They did not experience the "better things" in Christ.
    A. Faith apprehended Christ in prospect (v. 13)
    B. A desire for a "heavenly country" (vv. 15-16)
    C. Faith guaranteed receipt of the promise (vv. 39-40)

(from "Search the Scriptures")

Lesson Development

I. A TIME TO REMEMBER

The list of heroes in chapter 11 contains the names of those held in high honor by three great religious traditions: Christianity, Judaism, and Islam. Moses and Abraham, for example. Others, like Barak and Jephthah are almost unknown by the modern reader. It is evident that any understanding of Hebrews 11 is built on an awareness of the people who are highlighted in its verses.

As you begin your study of this chapter, take as much time as needed to get acquainted with each person. Don't presume you remember the story. Reread the Old Testament account. Listed below are the scripture references where you can find each one in the Bible. The notation may not include their whole story, but will give you a place to begin.

Abel: Gen. 4:1-16
Enoch: Gen. 5:18-24
Noah: Gen. 6:13-22
Abraham: Gen. 12:1-8, 22; 13:14
Sarah: Gen. 17:17-19; 21:1-7
Abraham/Isaac: Gen. 22:1-14
Isaac/Jacob & Esau: Gen. 27:1-40
Jacob: Gen. 47:27-31
Joseph: Gen. 50:22-26; Exod. 13:19

Moses: Exod. 2:1-10; 12:1-30
Rahab: Josh. 2:1-24; 6:23
Gideon: Judg. 6:1—7:25
Barak: Judg. 4:1-24
Samson: Judg. 13:1—16:31
Jephthah: Judg. 10:6—12:7
David: 1 Sam. 16:1-13
Samuel: 1 Sam. 1:19-28

There are a variety of ways to implement your Old Testament study. One of the following, or some combination, may be just the answer for you.

1. Homework assignments. Ask the members of your group to select one or more of the Bible personalities listed above. Between sessions they are to review the story and bring a short report to class.

2. Divide into small research groups during your Bible study. Assign the Old Testament characters to different groups for study and report.

3. As the leader, thoroughly familiarize yourself with each of the people named in Hebrews 11. Ask the group what they remember about each one. From your study, fill in any gaps in information so that the story will be complete.

You may want to write notes from your research in the space provided.

II. DISCUSSION QUESTIONS

1. In relation to verses 1-2, how do you react to the boy's comment, "Faith is believing what you know ain't so."

2. Is there any theory on how our world began that is not based on faith? Comment on your answer. (v. 3)

3. In what ways does a person continue to speak following his death? (v. 4)

4. When you combine verse 14 with Genesis 4:1-16, what conclusions can you make relative to Abel's faith?

5. According to verse 6, what two things must a person believe in order to please God?

6. When you read quickly through the first 16 verses, what single phrase has the greatest impact on you? Why?

7. Review verses 13-16. What do they teach about the length of time faith needs to remain active?

8. What is the difference between faith and hope, especially as the words are used in Hebrews 11?

9. From your review of the persons named in Hebrews 11, formulate answers to these questions:

   a. Why, in your opinion, was each one selected for this Hebrew Hall of Fame?

   b. Are there significant differences between them in the operation and application of their faith? If yes, what are they?

   c. Are there different kinds of faith? For different purposes?

10. Verse 39 indicates that their faith was incomplete. How was it unfinished? How are we involved?

III. PRAYER TIME

1. Take the time to share personal spiritual victory. Give special attention to recent answers to prayer.

2. Encourage the group to share their personal needs—special requests for prayer.

3. Volunteer, or assign, a prayer request to someone in the group as their spiritual responsibility during the next week.

4. Pray together for each other.

IV. SOMETHING TO THINK ABOUT OR DO

Select one of the key personalities of Hebrews 11. Study their life history in greater depth during the week allowing the Holy Spirit to guide and counsel you.

Read chapters 12 and 13 this week, asking the Holy Spirit to guide you in understanding their truths and applying them to your life.

12

The Disciplined Life

HEBREWS 11:39—13:25

Did you ever stand in quiet respect where national heroes are honored, perhaps at the Tomb of the Unknown Soldier in Arlington National Cemetery, or in the Peace Room in the Parliament Building in Ottawa, Canada? If you have, you instinctively know the meaning of the words, "Therefore, since we are surrounded by such a great cloud of witnesses, let us . . ." (12:1). Those who have given "the last full measure of devotion" challenge us to also give our best.

After having recounted the exploits of the great heroes of the faith, the writer says that "God had planned something better for us."

Incredible!

Yet, even that is not the end: "God had planned something better for *us so that only together with us would they be made perfect*" (11:40, italics added). As Christians, we are not meant to be disconnected units living fragmented, lonely lives in a hostile world. We are a part of a family, a part of the Body of Christ.

There is great joy in that realization. And tremendous responsibility! We not only receive, but we are called on to give to our brothers and sisters in Christ. To do that effectively we must grow beyond the elementary truths (6:1) and commit ourselves to a disciplined life—a life where faith and action are joyfully intertwined. The concluding portion of the Book of Hebrews sets forth the implications and instructions that flow from this great Christian truth.

Richard Taylor gives us this outline as a guide for our study:

I. The perseverance of faith (12:1-29)
   A. Resources in Christ (vv. 1-4)
   B. Incentives in chastening (vv. 5-11)
   C. Diligence in holiness (vv. 12-17)
   D. An awful ultimatum (vv. 18-29)
II. The way of faith (13:1-19)
   A. A way of practical holiness (vv. 1-7)
   B. A way of absolute loyalty (vv. 8-16)
   C. A way of humble submission (vv. 17-19)

III. Conclusion (13:20-25)
   A. A benedictory prayer (vv. 20-21)
   B. Personal greetings (vv. 22-25)

Lesson Development

I. A SUMMARY AND CHALLENGE

The inspired writer is pulling in the strands of truth that have run through the Epistle from the beginning. It is both summary and challenge.

Let us do the same: focus our primary study on this concluding portion, but drawing from all of our previous study in Hebrews for supporting verses. In group study you may want to divide into small committees for a period of study on these subjects, then come back together and share your findings.

Listed below are four main subjects found in this concluding section. Read 11:39—13:25 carefully to find everything the writer says about each theme. Reach back into your earlier study for additional verses that support or complement what is written here. Write down the truths you find. Be prepared to:

1. Share them with the group.

2. Discuss their implications for the 20th-century church.

3. Share anything new you have learned that will help you be a better Christian.

The four main ideas are: discipline, holiness (holy living), encouragement, words of advice. As you discover the answers to the questions listed below you will uncover the kernel of this beautiful concluding passage.

Discipline

1. To what, or whom, does the phrase, "a great cloud of witnesses" refer (v. 1)?

2. What advice is given about the preparation for, and participation in, the Christian race (vv. 1-3)?

3. What are some of the things that hinder spiritual growth in Christians?

4. What do these verses tell us about Christ?

5. Read verses 5-11. What message do they carry concerning discipline in the Christian life?

Holiness

Peace: a biblical term that means more than the absence of strife. It also carries the idea of health and wholeness.

Holiness: also known as entire sanctification, "A biblical term for the entire working of the Holy Spirit within our hearts whereby we are inwardly renewed and made free from sin" (W. T. Purkiser, BBC, vol. 10, p. 108).

1. React to this quotation, "For peace almost anything may be sacrificed, but not purity" (BBC, vol. 10, p. 107).
2. Why do you think the writer said that "without holiness no one will see the Lord" (v. 14)?
3. In what way does the example of Moses meeting God on Mount Sinai illustrate the New Testament teaching of Christian holiness (vv. 18-24)?
4. How does the experience of entire sanctification affect the family, friends, and associates of the person who experiences this grace from God (vv. 14-17)?

Encouragement and Words of Advice

Review what the writer has said in his closing remarks in chapter 13. Select two words of encouragement and two words of advice that our world needs to hear. Be prepared to present your selections to the group along with the reasons why you consider them to be important.

II. AN INTERLUDE FOR REFLECTION

1. What is the most important new truth you learned from this lesson?

2. What are the life-changing ideas you gained from this study in the Book of Hebrews?

III. PRAYER TIME

Share with one another your hopes for the future. Pray specifically for each member of the Bible study group.

"May the God of peace, who through the blood of the eternal covenant brought back from the dead our Lord Jesus, that great Shepherd of the sheep, equip you with everything good for doing his will, and may he work in us what is pleasing to him, through Jesus Christ, to whom be glory for ever and ever. Amen" (Hebrews 13:20-21).

Bibliography

Barclay, Willliam. "The Daily Study Bible Series," *The Letter to the Hebrews* (Philadelphia: Westminster Press, 1957).

Beacon Bible Commentary, volume 10 (Kansas City: Beacon Hill Press of Kansas City, 1967).

Beacon Bible Expositions, volume 11 (Kansas City: Beacon Hill Press of Kansas City, 1974).

Meyer, F. B. *The Way into the Holiest* (Grand Rapids: Zondervan Publishing House, 1953).

Search the Scriptures, New Testament, volume 14 (Kansas City: Nazarene Publishing House, 1958).

Wiley, H. Orton. *The Epistle to the Hebrews* (Kansas City: Beacon Hill Press, 1959).

Write for information about additional individual or small-group Bible study guides.

Beacon Hill Press of Kansas City
Box 527, Kansas City, MO 64141

NOTES: